ORACLE

FORMS
AND
REPORTS

Best 42 Oracle Reports Questions and Answers

Best 51 Oracle Forms Questions and Answers

Best 27 Common asked Questions in Interview

Table of Contents

Oracle Reports

Question 1: What is Oracle Developer?

Oracle Developer consists of Oracle Components that are helpful in designing the meaningful applications.

Question 2: What is a Report Builder?

Report Builder is a component of Oracle Developer that is used to display data in a specified format required by the user.

Question 3: What are the various styles used in the Reports?

Various styles used in Reports are:

a) Tabular

b) Form-Like

c) Mailing Label

d) Form Letter

e) Group Left

f) Group Above

g) Matrix

h) Matrix with Group

Question 4: What is GUI?

GUI stands for Graphical User Interface. GUI is a program interface that takes advantage of the computer's graphics Capabilities to make the program easier to use.

Question 5: What are the different Report Builder Components?

Report Builder Components are:

a) Object Navigator

b) Property palette

c) Data Model Editor

d) Layout Model Editor

e) Parameter Form Editor

Question 6: What is a difference between Object Navigator and property Palette?

The object navigator shows a hierarchical view of objects in the report and a property palette is a window that displays the settings for defining an oracle report object.

Question 7: What is a Syntax Palette?

Syntax palette is a programming tool that helps in copying the syntax of Constructs into the PL/SQL Editor.

Question 8: What are the different ways of viewing the Report output?

Different ways of viewing the Report output are:

a) Screen

b) Preview

c) Printer

d) Mail

e) File

f) Cache

g) Localfile

h) Sysout

Question 9: Can Report output to multiple destinations?

Yes, the Report can be Output to multiple Destinations in one single run of the Report.

Question 10: What is a difference between Screen view and Preview?

Use the Screen font to format. It does not consider printer fonts. Use the Printer font to format and Screen font to Display. Using Preview gives you a better impression of how the printed result will appear.

Question 11: What are the different types of Report Builder Modules?

Different types of Report Builder Modules are:

a) Reports

b) Templates

c) External SQL Queries

d) PL/SQL Libraries

Question 12: Explain different types of Report Builder Views?

Different types of Report Builder Views are:

a) Data Model

b) Layout Model

c) Live Previewer

d) Parameter Form

Data Model: Defines the Data structure and the values to be Displayed.

Layout model: Formatting Information about how the values appear in the Output.

Live Previewer: Displays Report Output and allows simple modifications to the Layout without having opened the Layout Model.

Parameter Form: Allows the user input values at runtime through runtime parameter values.

Question 13: Explain Report builder objects?

Report builder objects falls into following three categories:

Data model objects:

a) Query: defines the Data structure i.e. SQL Query.

b) Group: Each group is owned by a Query. Used to group columns selected in the query. Oracle Report automatically creates a group for each query.

c) Columns: consists of Formula, Summary and Placeholder columns.

d) Data Link: Join Queries for complex data relationships.

e) Parameter: consists of System and User Parameters.

Layout model objects:

a) Repeating Frame: Contains objects that can print once for each record of associated group.

b) Frame: Contains objects that can print only once.

c) Field: Contains data and other variable values and their format.

d) Boilerplate: Consists of general, text or graphics type.

Parameter form objects:

a) Field: Contains Parameter values.

b) Boilerplate: Contains constant text or graphics that appears on the runtime parameter form. Consists of graphical, text and image type.

Question 14: What are the different styles of breaking the reports?

There are two different styles of breaking the reports:

a) Group left

b) Group above

Question 15: Name three different templates options in report builder?

Three different templates (.tdf) options in report builder are:

a) Predefined Template

b) Template File (browse)

c) No Template

Question 16: What are the different ways to store Report builder module?

There are two different ways to store Report builder module:

a)   Operating System File

b)   Report Builder Database Table

Question 17: Where can you store Template module?

Template module can be stored in an operating system file only, not in the database tables.

Question 18: Explain different extensions of Reports?

Different extensions of Reports are:

a)   . Rdf: Binary mode, executable (Full Report definition is modifiable)

b)   . Rep: Binary mode, executable (not modifiable, no source code)

c)   . Rex: Contains ASCII text. Not executable.

Question 19: Give any one reason of saving the report builder module in the database?

One reason for saving in the database is to use the reports utility to document your Report definition.

Question 20: How can you convert your report definitions from one storage type to another?

You can convert your report definitions from one storage type (.rdf, .rep, .rex) to another by using RWCON60 executable.

Question 21: How many query and group do Tabular style, Group above and Group left prepares?

The objects that the report wizard creates by default depend on the style of report that you choose:

a)   Tabular Style: one query, one group

b)   Group Above, Group Left: one query, two or more groups.

Report Wizard creates only one Query.

Question 22: How can you delete a database column from the group?

You cannot delete a database column object directly from the group. To delete a column you must remove the corresponding expression from the SELECT statement in the Query.

Question 23: Do Report wizard supports page summaries?

Report Wizard does not support page summaries. Create the field manually in the Layout editor.

Question 24: What is the minimum number of groups in Matrix Report?

The minimum number of groups in Matrix Report is Four.

Question 25: Name the three sections of Layout model?

Three sections of Layout model are:

a)   Header Section

b)   Main Section

c)   Trailer Section

Question 26: What is a difference between Confine and Flex mode?

To avoid errors in Layout model always work in the layout using the Confine Mode and Flex Mode.

Confine Mode consist of:

a)   Close Padlock: Restrict to move objects position

b)   Open Padlock: Does not restrict to move objects.

Flex Mode consist of:

a)   Enabled: Layout boundary moves with the objects.

b)   Disabled: Only the object can move.

Question 27: What is an Anchor?

Anchor is used to position the object position in relative to another object. Anchor is also used for suppressing spaces.

Question 28: What are the advantages of using Button on Reports?

Button is used to perform additional actions such as:

1) Accessing a URL

2) Calling another report etc.

Question 29: What is Conditional Formatting?

Conditional formatting is a programming tool that is used to hide, change font, color etc of objects based on some conditions.

Question 30: Explain different types of columns used in report builder?

Different Columns contained in Report Builder are:

a) Data Columns

b) Formula Columns

c) Summary Columns

d) Placeholder Columns

Data Columns: Data Columns contain the data values for a report. Data Columns are corresponding to the table columns included in the select list of a query. Each column is placed in the group associated with the query.

Formula Columns: Formula Columns performs user-defined computations. Formula Columns executes a PL/SQL function and must return a value. Formula Columns can be placed at the Report or Query level. Formula Columns should not be used to set a parameter's value. Formula Columns is denoted by CF_

Summary Columns: Summary Columns are used for calculating summary information like: Sum, Average, Minimum, Maximum, Count, First, Last, % of Total, Std Deviation and Variance. Summary Columns can be placed at the Report or Query level. Summary Columns is denoted by CS_.

Placeholder Columns: Placeholder Columns are storage areas in the Data Model. Used for Temporary storage of data for future reference. Placeholder Columns value can be set in the following places: Before Report Trigger and Report-Level Formula Columns. Placeholder Columns can be populated by a Before Report Trigger but are generally populated by a Formula. Although Placeholders allow PL/SQL to be written within them, they cannot be Self-populated, their value must be set by an external program Unit and any attempts at self-population will result in a runtime compilation error. However the Formula assigned to the Placeholder must return a value. Placeholder Columns is denoted by CP_.

Example: At Formula column:

Function CF_1formula return Number is

Begin

If :no_in_stock<10 then

:CP_1:='Only'||:no_in_stock||'Items left in stock!!';

End if;

Return 1;

End;

Example at Placeholder column:

Function CP_1formula return Char is

Begin

Return null;

End;

Question 31: How many types of Report Builder Triggers are there?

There are five different types of Report Builder Triggers:

a)   Before Parameter Form

b)   After Parameter Form

c)   Before Report

d)   Between Pages

e)   After Report

Question 32: Explain Report Builder Triggers in detail?

Before Parameter Form fires before the Runtime Parameter Form is displayed. From this Trigger, you can access and change the value of parameters, PL/SQL Global variables and report-level columns. If the runtime parameter form is suppressed, this trigger still fires. This Trigger can be used for validation of command line parameters.

After Parameter Form fires after the Runtime Parameter Form is displayed. From this Trigger, you can access and check Parameter values. Is used to perform dynamic query through Lexical parameters. Columns from the Data Model are not accessible from this Trigger If the runtime parameter form is suppressed, this trigger still fires. This Trigger can be used for validation of command line parameters. Any processing that will affect the data retrieved by the report should be performed in these triggers (Before and After Parameter Form Triggers).These are the two triggers that fire before anything is parsed or fetched.

Before Report fires before the report is executed but after the query is parsed.

Between Pages fires before each page of the report is formatted, except the very first page. This trigger can be used for customised page formatting. In the previewer, the trigger only fires the first time that you go to a page. If you subsequently return to the page, the trigger does not fire again.

After Report fires after you exit the previewer, or after report output is sent to a specified destination, such as a file, printer etc. This trigger can be used to clean up any initial processing that was done such as deleting tables. This trigger always fires, whether or not your report completed successfully. Any processing that will not affect the data retrieved by the report can be performed in these triggers (Before, After report and between Pages).

Question 33: What is a Format Trigger? Explain in brief?

Format Trigger is used to format objects based on some conditions. Format trigger are PL/SQL functions executed before the object is displayed. The function must return a Boolean value (TRUE or FALSE). Format triggers do not affect the data retrieved by the report. Don't perform calculations or use DML in a format trigger because it cannot be sure how many times a format trigger will fire for a particular object. For example: Highlighting a value, Highlighting a row, Suppressing labels, Suppressing values, Placing commas between fields etc.

Question 34: What are Lexical Parameters?

Lexical Parameters performs dynamic SQL query. Use to change the data definition at runtime. Use Lexical references to replace the clauses appearing after SELECT, FROM, WHERE, GROUP BY, ORDER BY, HAVING, CONNECT BY, and START WITH. Is denoted by '&'. You cannot make lexical references in a PL/SQL statement. However, use a bind reference in PL/SQL to set the value of a parameter that is then referenced lexically in SQL. Code is written in AFTER PARAMETER FORM Trigger.

For example:

DATA MODEL QUERY:

Select * from employee where dept_id=10 &status-----lexical parameter

CODING AT AFTER PARAMETER FORM

Function AfterPForm return Boolean is

BEGIN

IF :status='ALL' Then

:status:='AND (STATUS IN ("P","N") OR STATUS IS NULL)';

ELSIF :status='P' Then

:status:='AND STATUS="P" ';

ELSE

Null;

END IF;

END;

Question 35: What is difference between Vertical and Horizontal Elasticity?

Vertical Elasticity property deals with how the vertical size of the object may change at runtime to accommodate the objects or data within it.

Vertical Elasticity is categorised into four properties:

a)   Contract: Means the vertical size of the object decreases. If the formatted objects or data within it are short enough, but it cannot increase to a height greater than that shown in the Report Editor. Truncation of data may occur.

b)   Expand: Means the vertical size of the object increases, if the formatted objects or data within it are tall enough, but it cannot decrease to a height less than that shown in the Report Editor.

c)   Fixed: Means the height of the object is the same on each logical page, regardless of the size of the objects or data within it. Truncation of data may occur.

d)   Variable: Means the object may expand or contract vertically to accommodate the objects or data within it (with no extra space).

Horizontal Elasticity property deals with how the horizontal size of the object may change at runtime to accommodate the objects or data within it.

Vertical Elasticity is categorised into four properties:

a)   Contract: Means the horizontal size of the object decreases. If the formatted objects or data within it are wide enough, but it cannot increase to a width greater than that shown in the Report Editor. Truncation of data may occur.

b)   Expand: Means the horizontal size of the object increases, if the formatted objects or data within it are wide enough, but it cannot decrease to a width less than that shown in the Report Editor.

c)   Fixed: Means the width of the object is the same on each logical page, regardless of the size of the objects or data within it. Truncation of data may occur.

d)   Variable: Means the object may expand or contract horizontally to accommodate the objects or data within it (with no extra space).

Question 36: What is difference between Page Break Before and page Break After?

Page Break before indicates that you want the object to be formatted on the page after the page on which it is initially triggered to print. Note that this does not necessarily mean that all the objects below the object with Page Break Before will move to the next page. Suppose that you want each instance of a repeating frame to be on a logical page by itself. First, set Maximum Records per Page to 1 for the repeating frame so that only one instance appears on each logical page. Then, specify Page Break Before and Page Break After, to make sure that the first instance of the repeating frame starts on a new logical page.

Page Break After property indicates that you want all children of the object to be moved to the next page. In other words, any object that is a child object of an anchor (implicit or explicit) to this object will be treated as if it has Page Break Before set to Yes. Note that this does not necessarily mean that all the objects below the object with Page Break After will move to the next page. Suppose that you want each instance of a repeating frame to be on a logical page by itself. First, set Maximum Records per Page to 1 for the repeating frame so that only one instance appears on each logical page. Then, specify Page Break Before and Page Break After, to make sure that the first instance of the repeating frame starts on a new logical page.

Question 37: What is Page Protect in Oracle Reports?

The Page Protect property indicates whether to try to keep the entire object and its contents on the same logical page. Setting Page Protect to yes means that if the contents of the object cannot fit on the current logical page, the object and all of its contents will be moved to the next logical page. Suppose that you have a group report. If at all possible, you would like to have all of the details and the master appearing on the same page. To do this, you specify Page Protect for the master repeating frame (the outermost repeating frame). If the details and the master cannot fit on the first page on which they are triggered to print, they will be triggered to print on the next page instead.

Question 38: What are the parameters of RUN_PRODUCT Procedure in Oracle Reports?

The Syntax of RUN_PRODUCT is:

RUN_PRODUCT (Product Number, Module Varchar2, Commmode Number, Execmode Number, Location Number, Paramlist_id Varchar2, Display Varchar2)

Product: Oracle product you want to invoke can be a Forms, Graphics, Reports, Book.

Module: Defines a Path from where to call a Product.

Commmode: Communication mode to be used when running the called product. Can be either:

a)   Synchronous: Specifies that control returns to form only after the called product has been exited. The end user cannot work in the form while the called product is running.

b)   Asynchronous: Specifies that control returns to the calling application immediately even if the called application has not completed its display.

Execmode: Execution mode to be used when running the called product. For Reports and Graphics Builder execmode can be either BATCH or RUNTIME. For Form Builder only RUNTIME is used.

Location: Location can be either FILE SYSTEM or the DATABASE.

Paramlist_Id: Specifies the Parameter list to be passed to the called Product.

Display: Used only for Graphics Builder. (Blockname.Item_name)

Question 39: What we use SRW Package in Oracle Reports?

Some of the uses of SRW Package are:

a)   SRW.DO_SQL

b)   SRW.RUN_REPORT

c)   SRW.MESSAGE

d)   SRW.PROGRAM_ABORT

e)   SRW.DO_SQL_FAILURE

Question 40: What is difference between Live Previewer and Runtime Preview?

The main difference between Live Previewer and Runtime Preview is as below:

	Live Previewer	Runtime Preview
1	Can open one at a time	Can Open many at once throughSRW.Run_Report Package defined at Button.
2	Can modify the layout without opening the layout Editor	Cannot modify the Layout.
3	Cannot magnifying or reduce the report O/P.	Can magnifying or reduce the report O/P.
4	Cannot split the report output horizontally or vertically	Can split the report output horizontally or vertically

Question 41: Explain System Parameters of Oracle Reports in detail?

The main System Parameters of Oracle Reports are:

a)   BACKGROUND: Is whether the report should run in the foreground or the background.

b)   COPIES: Is the number of report copies that should be made when the report is printed.

c)   CURRENCY: Is the symbol for the currency indicator (e.g., "$").

d)   DECIMAL: Is the symbol for the decimal indicator (e.g., ".").

e)   DESFORMAT: Is the definition of the output device's format (e.g., landscape mode for a printer). This parameter is used when running a report in a character-mode environment, and when sending a bitmap report to a file (e.g. to create PDF or HTML output).

f)   DESNAME: Is the name of the output device (e.g., the file name, printer's name, mail userid).

g)   DESTYPE: Is the type of device to which to send the report output (screen, file, mail, printer, or screen using PostScript format).

h)   MODE: Is whether the report should run in character mode or bitmap.

i)   ORIENTATION: Is the print direction for the report (landscape, portrait, default).

j)   PRINTJOB: Is whether the Print Job dialog box should appear before the report is run.

k)   THOUSANDS: Is the symbol for the thousand's indicator (e.g., ",").

Question 42: How can you create Additional Report Layout in Oracle Reports?

Additional Report Layout can be created by dragging an Additional Default Layout button from a tool palette in layout section.

Oracle Forms

Question 1: What is Form Builder?

Form builder is a component of Oracle Developer that is used to develop form based Applications for presenting and manipulating data.

Question 2: What is a difference between Frame, Item and Block?

Frame is used to arrange data block items. **Item** are Members of data block. Items grouped into Records. **Block** provides a mechanism for grouping related items into a functional unit for storing, displaying and manipulating Records.

Question 3: What is a difference between Window, Canvas and View Port?

Window is a container for all visual objects that make up a form application. Window performs functionality such as scrolling, moving and resizing. A single form may include several windows. Each window should have at least one content canvas. Each new form module has one predefined window which is called Window1 and is a modeless window.

Canvas is a surface inside a window on which visual objects can be placed. A canvas is assigned to a window. Each item in a form must refer to not more than one canvas.

View port is a visible portion of canvas.

Question 4: What is MDI?

MDI (Multiple Document Interface) is a parent window through which multiple documents can be accessed and browsed.

Question 5: What is a difference between Modal and Modeless window?

Modal Window is a restricted window that requires a window exit before moving to another window. You cannot move freely between windows. **Modeless Window** is an unrestricted window that the user can move freely. User can have simultaneously access to more than one window.

Question 6: What are Canvases in Oracle Forms and describe different types of Canvases?

Canvas is a surface inside a window on which visual objects can be placed. A canvas is assigned to a window. Each item in a form must refer to not more than one canvas.

Types of Canvases:

1) Content Canvas

2) Stacked Canvas

3) Toolbar Canvas

a) Vertical Toolbar

b) Horizontal toolbar

4) Tab Canvas

Content Canvas is a base canvas and is a default canvas type. Content canvas occupies the entire content area of the window. More than one content canvas can be assigned to the same window but only one content canvas can be displayed on a window at a time. To display more than one content canvas at the same time, assign each content canvas to a different window.

Stacked Canvas is displayed on top of the content canvas and is usually small in size then that of content canvas in the same window. To convert an existing content canvas to a stacked canvas, simply change its canvas type property from content to stack. To show and hide canvases programmatically, use the SHOW_VIEW, HIDE_VIEW and SET_VIEW_PROPERTY built-ins. stacked canvas is useful to display additional information, for hiding information and can act as a scrolling view.

Toolbar Canvas is used to create toolbar for individual window. Toolbar canvas is of two types: Vertical and Horizontal toolbar canvases.

Vertical Toolbar canvas is displayed to the left of a content canvas. **Horizontal Toolbar canvas** is displayed at the top of a content canvas. Toolbar canvas is used to hold buttons and other frequently used GUI elements. Toolbar canvas increases application usability and decrease form module maintenance Time. Object Navigator window has both horizontal and vertical toolbars where as Property Palette has a horizontal toolbar only. You can also create more than one toolbar for the same window. **MDI Toolbar:** Attaching a Toolbar to a form provides a MDI toolbar, so that there is no need to create more than one toolbar for a form application that uses multiple windows. Toolbar can be attached to individual windows or to the form itself.

Tab Canvas enables the user to organize and display data on separate Tabs. Tab canvas is displayed on top of the Content Canvas. Each Tab canvas is made up of one or more **Tab pages** and must have at least one. Each Tab page occupies an equal amount of space on Tab canvas. Any Item you place on a Tab canvas has a Canvas property as well as Tab page Property. The ordering of Tab pages in the object navigator determines the left-to-right or Top-To-bottom order of the Tabs at runtime. Tab canvas provides easy access to data and displays large amount of data on a single canvas and is also used to hide information.

Question 7: What are Messages and Alerts?

Messages and Alerts are the form of communication between the application and the User.

Types of Messages:

1) Informative message

2) Error message

3) Working message

4) Application message

Informative Message informs the user about the current state of processing. Example: Last value retrieved Press [Accept] to enter answer. Informative messages can be suppressed with an On-Message Trigger.

Error Message informs the user about the errors interrupting the processing. Example: Function key not allowed. Press [Show function keys] for list of valid keys too many arguments on command line. Error messages can be suppressed with an On-Error Trigger.

Working Message informs the operator that the form is currently in processing. Example: Working... Working message can be suppressed by setting the system variable SUPPRESS_WORKING to True.Example: Sytem.suppress_working: ='TRUE'

Application Message is created by the programmer using the MESSAGE built-in.

Types of Alerts:

1) System Alert

2) Application Alert

Alerts are displayed in a Modal window.

System Alert is a system acknowledgement to the operator before processing can be continue.

Application Alert are designed and created by the programmer as part of application using SHOW_ALERT built-in.

Question 8: Explain Message Severity level in Oracle Forms?

Message Severity Level is used to suppress messages according to the severity level. There are six different severity levels that the programmer can affect: 0, 5, 10, 15, 20, and 25. The default value is 0 for all messages. If the severity level is greater than 25 than the Message cannot be suppressed. During a run form session, form builder suppresses all messages with severity levels that are the same or lower than the indicated severity level. Defined with: system.message_level. Form builder does not suppress prompts or vital error messages, no matter what severity level you select.

Question 9: When can the Triggers in oracle forms can be failed?

Triggers are failed only when one of the following occurs:

a)   During an Unhandled exception

b)   By raising built-in exception FORM_TRIGGER_FAILURE. Means failing a trigger in a controlled manner.

c)   FORM_TRIGGER_FAILURE is a predefined Pl/Sql exception available only in form Builder.

Question 10: What is a difference between ON-ERROR and ON-MESSAGE Trigger?

ON-ERROR Trigger fires whenever an Oracle Forms causes an error message to display. ON-ERROR Trigger is used to replace default error message with a customized   Message. Built-in functions that are used to determine the Error message are: ERROR_CODE, ERROR_TEXT, ERROR_TYPE (FRM, ORA).

ON-MESSAGE Trigger fires whenever an Oracle Forms causes a message to   display. ON-MESSAGE Trigger is used to replace default message with a customized   Message. Built-in functions that are used to determine the message are: MESSAGE_CODE, MESSAGE_TEXT, MESSAGE_TYPE (FRM, ORA, NULL).

Question 11: Name the types of Alert properties?

Types of Alert properties are: Stop, Caution and Note.

Question 12: What are Input items? Explain different types of Input items?

Input Items are those items that accepts user Input. Input items enables insert, update, delete or query an item process.

Types of Input Items:

Check Box is a two-state interface object that indicates whether a certain value is Checked or unchecked. Trigger associated with check box is WHEN-CKECKBOX-CHANGED.

WHEN-CHECKBOX-CHANGED:This Trigger fires whenever an operator changes the state of a check box, either by clicking with the mouse or through keyboard interaction.

List Item consists of many alternative choices, out of which one and only one can be selected at a time. There are three types of list item: Poplist, Tlist and Combo Box. Poplist is a field with an iconic button attached to the right side. When user clicks on   a poplist, all of its elements are displayed. Tlist appears as a rectangular box that displays the list elements. Scroll bar appears to the right side of the list, if the list is bigger.

Combo box accepts user input. Appears as a field with a down arrow next to its right side. Trigger associated with list item is WHEN-LIST-CHANGED. WHEN-LIST-CHANGED Trigger fires when an operator selects a different element in a list item or de-selects the currently selected element. In addition, if a When-List-Changed trigger is attached to a combo box style, it fires each time the operator enters or modifies the entered text.

Radio Group consists of a fixed number of radio button options and only one can be selected at a time. It is alternative to List item. Consider List Item instead of Radio Group if there are more than four or five choices. Trigger associated with Radio Group is WHEN-RADIO-CHANGED. WHEN-RADIO-CHANGED Trigger fires when an operator selects a different Radio button in a radio group or de-selects the currently selected radio button either by clicking with the mouse or through keyboard interactions.

Question 13: What are Non-Input items? Explain its types?

Non-Input Items are those items that do not accept direct user input.

Types of Non-Input items:

Display Item is a read-only text item. Display item is similar to text item except that it cannot not be edited, queried, Navigated or accepts user input.

Image Item is used to store and display images. User can populate an image item either by fetching from a LONG RAW or BLOB Column or by using a trigger and a built-in to populate the image item programmatically. Images can be stored in either the database or the file system. When user insert images into the database by means of a save (commit), they are automatically compressed using the Oracle image compression. Images can also be populated with a BFILE, but will need to use DBMS_LOB to do so. Images cannot be cached. Triggers associated with the image item are: WHEN-IMAGE-ACTIVATED, WHEN-IMAGE-PRESSED. WHEN-

IMAGE-ACTIVATED Trigger fires whenever an operator selects or de-selects the image item. WHEN-IMAGE-PRESSED Trigger fires whenever an operator single-click or double-click on an image item.

Push Button Push Button is a non-input item that does not store or display data. Push Button is an interface object that is clicked to initiate an action. It is used for: Navigating between items, Display an LOV, Invoke an editor, calling to another window, Commit the data, Issue a query, Perform Calculations. Trigger associated with the Push Button is: WHEN –BUTTON-PRESSED.WHEN-BUTTON-PRESSED Trigger fires when an operator selects a button either by way of key or by clicking with a mouse.

Calculated Items are read-only items that are used for performing calculations. Can be expressed as: **Formula Calculated Item:** Performs horizontal calculations. Involves bind variables. **Summary calculated Item:** Performs Vertical calculations on values of a single item over all rows in a block.

Hierarchical Tree Items displays data in the form of standard Navigator style.

Bean Area Item enables you to integrate JAVA components into your application.

JAVA Bean is a component written in JAVA that can plug into any applet or JAVA application. JAVA Beans helps to interact with the client machine.

Question 14: What are Relations in Oracle Forms and explain its types?

Relations involve the Master-Detail relationship. Relation can be build automatically through Data block wizard or manually through create toolbar.

Types of Relations:

Non-Isolated Relation is a default Type. Prevent the deletion of master record if the associated child record exists in the database. Default Triggers type that are created by this relation are: ON-CLEAR-DETAILS (Form-level), ON-POPULATE-DETAILS (Block-level), ON-CHECK-DELETE-MASTER (Block-level).

Isolated Relation allows the master record deletion if the associated child record exists. Default Triggers type that are created by this relation are: ON-CLEAR-DETAILS (Form-level), ON-POPULATE-DETAILS (Block-level).

Cascading Relation allows the deletion of child record if the associated master record is deleted. Default Triggers type that are created by this relation are: ON-CLEAR-DETAILS (Form-level), ON-POPULATE-DETAILS (Block-level), PRE-DELETE (Block-level).

The default program units (procedures) created for above all three types of Relations are the same: CHECK_PACKAGE_FAILURE, CLEAR_ALL_MASTER_DETAILS, and QUERY_MASTER_DETAILS.

Question 15: What is Co-ordination Causing Event? Explain different types of Co-ordination?

Any event that changes the current record in a Master block is a Co-ordination Causing Event.

Types of Co-ordination:

1) Deferred

2) Automatic Query

Three Conditions for coordination causing event are:

1) Immediate (Deferred=NO, Automatic Query=NO)

2) Deferred (Deferred=YES, Automatic Query=NO)

3) Deferred with Automatic Query (Deferred=YES, Automatic Query=YES)

Immediate: When the coordination-causing event occurs, Form builder fetches the detail record immediately.

Deferred: When the coordination-causing event occurs, the Form Builder has to navigate to the detail Block and executes the query in order to fetch the detail records.

Deferred with Automatic Query:

When the coordination-causing event occurs, the Form Builder has to navigate to the Detail Block in order to fetch the detail records.

Question 16: What are the two phases of block coordination?

Two phases of block coordination are:

Clear Phase: During the clear phase Oracle forms navigates internally to the detail block and fetches the detail records.

Population Phase: During a population phase Oracle forms issue a select statement to repopulate the detail records associated with the new master record.

Question 17: What are Editors? Explain different types of editors in oracle forms?

Editors are used for special requirements such as: larger editing window, Search/Replace, cut, copy, paste etc.

Types of Editors:

1) Default Editor

2) System Editor

3) User-Named Editor

Default Editor: The default editor provides standard editing features, including search/replace and cut, copy, and paste. The default editor is built into every form and is automatically available from every text item.

System Editor: If there is a system editor available, you can specify that Form Builder should use the current system editor, rather than the default editor.

User-Named Editor: Is a named object. You can specify editor attributes such as Window display size, Position and Title.

Built-in used for Editor:

SHOW-EDITOR: Is a built-in procedure, which accepts any editor name and takes some I/P string and returns modified O/P string.

EDIT_TEXTITEM: Needs the input focus to be in the text item before the built-in is executed.

Question 18: What is a LOV? Explain its types?

LOV (List of Values): An LOV is a scrollable popup window with either single or multi-column selection list.

Types of LOV:

Static LOV: Contains the predetermined values.

Dynamic LOV: Contains values that come at runtime.

LOV for Validation property of an item:

When LOV for validation is set to true, Oracle forms compares the current value of the Text item to the values in the first column displayed in the LOV whenever the Validation event occurs. If the value in the text item matches one of the values in the first column of LOV, validation succeeds, the LOV is not displayed and the processing continues normally. If the value in the text item does not match one of the values in the first column of the LOV, Oracle forms displays the LOV and uses the Text item value as the search criteria to automatically reduce the list.

Built-in used to display the LOV are: SHOW_LOV (Function), LIST_VALUES (Procedure). Built-in that is used for setting the LOV properties: SET_LOV_PROPERTY, GET_LOV_PROPERTY.

Question 19: What are Property Classes?

A Property Class is a named object that contains a list of properties and their settings. There can be any number of properties in a property class and the properties in a class can apply to different types of objects. Property Class can be subclass in any number of modules. Property Class can have Triggers. You can define a Trigger in a property class when you want a form, block or item that you base on the class to inherit the trigger. When you define a trigger in a property class, the trigger appears in the object navigator under the trigger node for the class, but does not appear under the trigger node for objects based on the class.

Question 20: What are the various different types of Properties in Oracle Forms?

The various different types of Properties in Oracle Forms are:

Default Property: Is the default property of an object. Is denoted by a circle.

Changed Property: When changing the default property value of an object to some new value. Is denoted by a square.

Inherited Property: Is one that takes its value from the property class. It is displayed with an arrow to the left of the property name.

Variant Property: Changes a value of inherited property results to a variant property. It is displayed with a red cross over an arrow.

Question 21: What are Visual Attributes?

Visual Attributes are the font, color and pattern properties that can be set for form and Menu objects. Visual Attributes includes the Font Properties such as Font name, font size, font style Font width etc. and color or pattern properties such as foreground color, background Color, Fill pattern etc.

Question 22: What is an Object Group?

Object Group is used to package related Form Builder objects so that they can be copied or used in another module. Example: You might build a appointment scheduler in a form and then decide to make it available from other forms in your applications. The scheduler would probably be built from several types of objects, including a window, canvas, blocks and items that display dates and appointments and, Triggers that contain the logic for scheduling and other functionality. If you packaged these objects into an object group, you could then copy them to any number of other forms in one simple operation. You can create object groups in form and menu modules. Once you create an object group, you can add and remove objects to it as desired. Dragging a block into an object group implicitly includes all objects that are contained within that block. (Items, triggers, relations etc.). The objects in a group must all be defined in the same module, you cannot place objects from two different forms in the same object group. An object group cannot contain another object group. When an object in an object group is deleted from a module, it is removed from the object group automatically. Deleting an object group from a module does not delete the objects it contains from the module.

Question 23: What is a Record Group?

Record Group defines the data structure that is used to represent LOV and also used to exchange data between forms. A record group can have an unlimited number of columns of type CHAR, NUMBER, or DATE provided that the total number of columns does not exceed 64K. Record Group column names cannot exceed 30 characters. Record Group is local to Form Builder, rather than existing in the Database.

Question 24: Explain different types of Record Groups?

Different types of Record Groups are:

Query Record Group has an associated Select statement and is derived from the Database table.

Non-Query Record Group does not associate with the Query and its structure and values can be modified programmatically at runtime. Non-Query Record Group can be created and modified only at runtime.

Static Record Group does not associated with Query, instead can define its structure and row values at design time and they remain fixed at runtime. Static Record Group can be created and modified only at design time.

Question 25: What is a difference between Object and PL/SQL Libraries?

Object Libraries are the collection of Form objects that can be used in other modules. Can contain simple objects, property classes, object groups and program units.

PL/SQL Libraries are the collection of PL/SQL Program units including procedures, Functions and packages whose code can be referenced and called from other modules.

Question 26: What are Smart Classes?

Smart Class is an object in an object library that is frequently used as a class.

Question 27: What is OC4J?

OC4J stands for Oracle Containers for J2EE. OC4J is preferred to run form applications. Oracle connectivity with JAVA is done through OC4J. On NT, run Batch file to start (startinst.bat) or stop (stopinst.bat) OC4J. OC4J starts in DOS Window. Minimize the window in order to work; closing the window will abort OC4J.

Question 28: What is a Console?

Console provides information at Runtime. Console consists of: Message line and Status line. **Message Line:** The Message line displays both form and application messages. **Status Line:** The Status Line displays a variety of Indicators to reflect the current status of the Form Module. Such as: Record n/m, enter-query, List of values etc.

Question 29: What is a difference between OPEN_FORM, CALL_FORM and NEW_FORM?

OPEN_FORM: OPEN_FORM opens another form in a modeless window. The user can work on multiple forms concurrently. The user can navigate within multiple forms. With the OPEN_FORM the user can call another form in a different database session. Syntax: OPEN_FORM ('form_name', active_mode, session_mode, data_mode, paramlist); default: activate and no session mode. OPEN_FORM is a restricted procedure and cannot be called in the Enter-Query mode.

CALL_FORM: CALL_FORM calls another form in a Modal window. The user cannot navigate within different Forms. Requires to exit the called form before navigating back to the calling form. Forms are called in the same session.

NEW_FORM: NEW_FORM exits the current form and opens the new form as a parent window. NEW_FORM releases the memory by exiting the current form.

Question 30: What are the benefits of multiple form Applications?

Benefits of Multiple form Applications are:

1. Easier to debug small form.
2. Flexibility between forms.
3. Easy to maintain.
4. Modularity.
5. Data can be exchanged between forms.

Question 31: Explain different methods for exchanging data between forms?

Data can be exchanged between forms by four different means:

1) Through Global variables

2) Through Parameter Lists

3) Through Global Record Groups

4) Through PL/SQL variables in shared libraries.

Through Global Variables: Global variables contain character data values with a maximum of 255 characters. Each Global variable is known by the same name to each form in the session.

Can be created by a PL/SQL assignment, or by the DEFAULT_VALUE built-in. Example :GLOBAL.cust.id, DEFAULT_VALUE ('','GLOBAL.cust_id). If the Global variable has not been initialized before it is referenced in a called form an error is reported.In order to ensure the existence of global variable use the DEFAULT_VALUE built-in. To remove default_value built-in use ERASE built-in. Ex: ERASE ('global_name').

Through Parameter Lists: Parameter can be of any data type. The use of parameters in Multi-form applications is limited by the fact that they are visible only to the form in which they are defined. The built-in OPEN_FORM optionally takes as an argument the name or id of a parameter list. The Built-ins that enable the user to work with parameter lists includes: GET_PARAMETER_LIST, CREATE_PARAMETER_LIST, DESTROY_PARAMETER_LIST, ADD_PARAMETER, DELETE_PARAMETER. Example: Parameter.cust_id.

Through Global Record Groups: To use Global Record Group:-

1)   Use CREATE_GROUP_FROM_QUERY to create the record group with Global_scope.

2)   Populate the Record Group with the POPULATE_GROUP built-in.

3)   The Record Group is now available to any form in the same session.

Through PL/SQL Variable in Shared Libraries: PL/SQL Variable use less memory than Global Variables. PL/SQL Variable can be of any Data Type.

To use PL/SQL variables:

1)   Create a PL/SQL Library.

2)   Create a package specification with variables.

3)   Attach the library to multiple forms.

4)   Set Variable values in calling form.

5)   OPEN_FORM with SHARE_LIBRARY_DATA option.

6)   Use variables in opened form.

Example: OPEN_FORM ('called_lib', Activate, No_session, Share_library_data)

Question 32: Explain EXIT_FORM in Oracle Forms?

EXIT_FORM Built-in is used for closing or exiting the form.

Syntax: EXIT_FORM   (ASK_COMMIT   or   DO_COMMIT   or   NO_COMMIT or NO_VALIDATE)

ASK_COMMIT: IS a default type. Gives the decision to the user.

DO_COMMIT: Posts and commit changes across all form for the current transaction.

NO_COMMIT: Validates and rollback uncommitted changes in the current form.

NO_VALIDATE: Is the same as NO_COMMIT but without validation.

Question 33: How code between forms can be shared?

Codes between forms can be shared through the followings:

1)   Library Modules by attaching them to each form as required.

2)   Stored Program Units in the database.

Question 34: Explain SYNCHRONIZE Built-in?

SYNCHRONIZE built-in is used to synchronize the Terminal Screen with the internal   State of the form. SYNCHRONIZE update the screen display to reflect the information that Form Builder has its internal representation of the screen.

Example:

BEGIN

FOR J IN 1..1000 LOOP

:Control.Id:=J;

SYNCHRONIZE;

Process_Element(J);

END LOOP;

END;

Question 35: What is a difference between Data and Control Block?

DATA BLOCK: Data Block is directly associated with the Database. This enables the user to automatically access and manipulates data in the database. Data Block is associated with either a

Database Table (or View), a stored procedure, A From clause query, or Transactional triggers. Items in the data block are called data items or base table items.

CONTROL BLOCK: Control Block is created manually, they are not associated with the Database. Items in the Control Block are called Control items.

Question 36: What is a Debugger?

With the Debugger you can monitor the execution of code within the trigger and other program units. The steps include:

1) **Step Into:** Executes the next statement.

2) **Step Over:** Executes the next statement without stepping into a nested subprogram.

3) **Step Out:** completes the nested subprogram and steps to the next executable statement in the calling program.

4) **Go:** resumes execution until the program terminates normally or is interrupted by the next breakpoint.

5) **Pause:** Pauses the execution of running PL/SQL code to enable you to examine the environment. For Example, you could check variable values.

6) **Stop:** Terminates debugging and program execution completely.

Question 37: What is an Indirect Reference?

Items can be referenced indirectly with the NAME_IN and COPY built-in Subprograms. Use Indirect referencing when you create procedures and functions in a library Module, because direct references cannot be resolved.

Question 38: What is a difference between NAME-IN and COPY built-in?

NAME-IN built-in (function): Returns the value of the indicated variable. The returned value is in the form of a character string. Use conversion functions for Number and Date. The NAME_IN function cannot return the contents of a global or local variable. In PL/SQL triggers that will be executed in enter_query mode, you must use NAME_IN rather than normal bind-variable notation to access values in the data-block. Bind variables cannot be referenced directly in the PL/SQL statements.

Example 1:

IF :emp.ename='abc'----Direct Reference

IF NAME_IN('emp.ename')='abc'----Indirect Reference

Example 2:

Date_var:=TO_DATE(NAME_IN('order.date_item'));

Num_var:=TO_NUMBER(NAME_IN('order.number_item'));

COPY built-in (Procedure): The COPY built-in assigns an indicated value to an indicated variable or item. The COPY built-in is used for copying a value from one item or variable into another item or global variable. Use COPY built-in because you cannot use standard PL/SQL syntax to set a referenced item equal to a value.

Example 1:

:emp.ename:='abc'---------Direct Reference

COPY('abc','emp.ename');----Indirect Reference

Example 2:

COPY('abc',NAME_IN('control.ref_name'));

Question 39: What is allowed and not allowed in Enter-Query Mode?

Enter-Query Mode Allows:

1)   Retrieve all Records

2)   Retrieve records by using selection criteria.

Enter-Query Mode does not Allows:

1)   Navigate out of the current block

2)   Exit from the runtime session

3)   Use certain functions such as Next Record.

4)   Insert new records

5)   Updating existing records

6)   Deleting Records.

Question 40: What is a Menu Module in Oracle Forms?

Menu Module consists of a hierarchy of menus, each with selectable items.

Question 41: Explain ONETIME_WHERE property?

For instances where you want to restrict the query only once, you can programmatically set the ONETIME_WHERE property of a block.

Example:

Set_Block_Property('INVENTORIES',
ONETIME_WHERE,'product_id='||:order_items.product_id);

Go_Block('INVENTORIES');

Execute_Query;

Question 42: What are the different methods of Navigation in Oracle Forms?

Different methods of Navigation are:

1)   Default Menu

2)   Menu Toolbar

3)   Mouse

4)   Buttons

5)   Function Keys

Question 43: What is a sequence of firing Triggers at Form level in Oracle Forms?

Sequences of firing Triggers at form level:

1)   PRE-LOGON

2)   ON-LOGON

3)   POST-LOGON

4)   PRE-FORM

5)   PRE-BLOCK

6)   WHEN-NEW-FORM-INSTANCE

7)   WHEN-NEW-BLOCK-INSTANCE

8) WHEN-NEW-ITEM-INSTANCE

9) POST-BLOCK

10) POST-FORM

Question 44: What is a sequence of firing Triggers at Item level in Oracle Forms?

Sequence of firing Triggers at Item level:

1) PRE-TEXT-ITEM

2) WHEN-NEW-ITEM-INSTANCE

3) KEY-NEXT-ITEM

4) POST-CHANGE

5) WHEN-VALIDATE-ITEM

6) POST-TEXT-ITEM

Question 45: What are the different types of Form builder variables?

Different types of Form builder variables are:

1) Item (:block_name.item_name)

2) Global (:GLOBAL.variable_name)

3) System (:SYSTEM.variable_name)

4) Parameter (:PARAMETER.name).

Question 46: What are the standard validation checks for Text item?

Standard validation checks for Text Item are:

1) Format mask

2) Required

3) Data Type

4) Lowest-Highest allowed Value

5)   Validate from List

Question 47: Explain Defer Requirement Enforcement?

This property applies only when item-level validation is in effect. When DRE is set to   Yes than WHEN-ITEM-VALIDATION Trigger does not fire. That is Item Level validation does not take place, then the error will be tracked during record-level validation.

Question 48: Explain the benefits of reusing objects and code in Oracle Forms?

Benefits of reusing objects and code are:

1)   Increase Productivity: Reusing objects and code decreases development time, thereby increasing productivity.

2)   Decrease Maintenance: Changing the code at one place reflects at many other places, thereby reducing maintenance time.

3)   Increase modularity: Sharing and reusing code increases the modularity of the applications.

4)   Maintain Standards: Standard objects and code can be used for multiple form modules.

5)   Improved Application Performance: By decreasing Network Traffic.

Question 49: Explain Triggers in Oracle Forms? Also explain different categories of Triggers?

Triggers are blocks of PL/SQL code that is written to perform some specific tasks. Trigger is a program unit that is executed or fired due to an event. Triggers can be fired for events such as:

1)   Query-related events

2)   During validation or navigation events

3)   For error or messages

4)   During Post or Commit process etc.

Trigger consists of three components:

1)   **Trigger Type:** Events that causes the Trigger to fire. (Pre, Post, When, On, Key Events).

2)   **Trigger Code:** Defines the action that Trigger should perform.

3)   **Trigger Scope:** Defines the level of the Trigger (Form, Block or Item level)

Pre-Event: Fires before an action is performed.

Post-Event: Fires just after an action has performed.

When-Event: Fires in addition to standard Processing. Is used to augment functionality. **On-Event:** Fires in place of standard processing. Used to replace or bypass a process. Also used for suppressing errors and messages.

Key-Triggers: Fires in place of standard action of a function key. Fires when the operator presses the associated key or key-sequence.

Trigger is divided into following categories:

1) Block Processing Triggers: When-Clear-Block, When-Create-Record, When-Database-record, When-Remove-Record.

2) Interface Event Triggers: When-Button-Pressed, When-Checkbox-Changed, When-Radio-Changed, When-List-Changed, When-Image-Activated, When-Image-Pressed, When-Mouse-Click, When-Mouse-DoubleClick, When-Mouse-Down, When-Mouse-up, When-Mouse-Move, When-Mouse-Enter, When-Mouse-Leave, When-Timer-Expired, When-Window-Activated, When-Window-Closed, When-Window-Deactivated, When-Window-Resized.

3) Key Triggers: Function Key, Key-Fn, Key-Others.

4) Master-Detail Triggers: On-Check-Delete-Master, On-Clear-Details, On-Populate-Details.

5) Message-Handling Triggers: On-Error, On-Message.

6) Navigational Triggers: Pre-Form, Pre-Block, Pre-Record, Pre-Text-Item, Post-Form, Post-Block, Post-Record, Post-Text-Item, When-Form-Navigate, When-New-Form-Instance, When-New-Block-Instance, When-New-Record-Instance, When-New-Item-Instance.

7) Query-Time Triggers: Pre-Query, Post-Query.

8) Transactional Triggers: On-Check-Unique, On-Close, On-Commit, On-Count, On-Fetch, On-Select, On-Delete, On-Insert, On-Update, On-Logon, On-Logout, On-Rollback, Post-Change, Post-Database-Commit, Post-Forms-Commit, Post-Delete, Post-Insert, Post-Update, Post-Select, Post-Fetch, Pre-Delete, Pre-Update, Pre-Insert, Pre-Commit, Pre-Select, Pre-Logon, Pre-Logout.

9) Validation Triggers: When-Validate-Item, When-Validate-Record.

10) User-Named Triggers: Execute_Trigger('Trigger_name')

Question 50: What are System Variables?

System variables are oracle form variables that are used to control the way an aplication behaves.

List of system Variables:

1) System.Form_Status

2) System.Block_Status

3) System.Record_Status

4) System.Coordination_Operation

5) System.Master_Block

6) System.Current_Block

7) System.Current_Form

8) System.Current_Item

9) System.Current_Value

10) System.Cursor_Block

11) System.Cursor_Record

12) System.Cursor_Item

13) System.Cursor_Value

14) System.Last_Form

15) System.Last_Record

16) System.Last_Query

17) System.Message_Level

18) System.Suppress_Working

19) System.Mode

Question 51: What is a difference between Restricted and Unrestricted Built-In Subprograms?

Built-in Subprogram is divided into two categories:

1) Restricted Built-in Subprograms

2) Unrestricted Built-in Subprograms

Restricted Built-In Subprograms:Restricted built-ins affect navigation in your form, either external screen navigation, or internal navigation. You can call these built-ins only from triggers where no internal navigation is occurring. Restricted built-ins cannot be called from the Pre and Post triggers, which fire when Oracle Forms is navigating from object to another. Restricted built-ins can be called from the When triggers that are specific to interface items, such as When-Button-Pressed or When-Checkbox-Changed. Restricted built-ins can also be called from any of the When-New-"Object"-Instance **triggers and from key triggers.** Examples: Clear_Block, Go_Block, Next_Block, Previous_Block, Clear_Form, Commit_Form, Enter, Exit_Form, Open_form etc.

Unrestricted Built-In Subprograms: Unrestricted built-ins do not affect logical or physical navigation and can be called from any Trigger. Examples:

1)   Show_Alert

2)   Pause

3)   Set and Get Built-ins (Ex: Get_Item_Property, Set_Item_Property)

4)   Find Built-ins (Ex: Find_Block, Find_View etc)

5)   Call_Form etc.

Common Questions Asked During Interview

Question 1: Please introduce yourself?

Question 2: Tell us something about your family background?

Question 3: Why there is an education gap (if any)?

Question 4: Why there is an experience gap (if any)?

Question 5: What are your current roles and responsibilities?

Question 6: Explain your role in current project?

Question 7: What challenges you faced in your current project?

Question 8: What else you think you have learnt or achieved from your current project?

Question 9: Who assign you the task and how you get it?

Question 10: Have you ever worked in tight deadlines?

Question 11: By what way you communicate to your client?

Question 12: How was your relation with your project manager?

Question 13: Apart from your job what extra you are working upon on getting exposure?

Question 14: Why do you want to leave your current organization?

Question 15: What do you know about our organization?

Question 16: Why should we hire you?

Question 17: What is your aim in life?

Question 18: Where do you want to see yourself after 5 years?

Question 19: What are your strengths?

Question 20: What are your weaknesses?

Question 21: What are your hobbies?

Question 22: What are your expectations from us?

Question 23: Are you ready to relocate?

Question 24: How soon can you join us?

Question 25: Are you ready to sign a bond/contract with us?

Question 26: What package are you expecting from us and is it negotiable?

Question 27: Any questions you want to ask from us related to organization, your role etc.?